Everyday Cupcakes

Everyone loves cupcakes. Even simple, everyday ones, like the ones listed below, are elegant and pretty, and very, very tasty. Your family will love these!

Entertaining & Parties

Cupcakes are made for parties! Whether you are holding a children's party, a tea party for you friends or a proper grown-up party, these cupcakes will go fast!

FLAME TREE has been creating family-friendly, classic and beginner recipes for our bestselling cookbooks for over 12 years now. Our mission is to offer you a wide range of expert-tested dishes, while providing clear images of the final dish so that you can match it to your own results. We hope you enjoy this super selection of recipes – there are plenty more to try! Titles in this series include:

Cupcakes • Slow Cooker • Curries Chinese • Soups • Baking Breads Cakes • Simple Suppers • Pasta Chicken • Fish & Seafood • Chocolate

For more information please visit:
www.flametreepublishing.com

Lemon Drizzle Cupcakes

INGREDIENTS

Makes 12 deep cupcakes or 18 fairy cakes

150 g/5 oz butter, softened
150 g/5 oz caster sugar
3 medium eggs, beaten
150 g/5 oz self-raising flour
½ tsp baking powder
1 lemon

To decorate:

1 lemon
50 g/2 oz caster sugar

1. Preheat the oven to 180°C/350°F/Gas Mark 4 and line a 12-hole muffin tray with paper cases, or two bun trays with 18 fairy-cake paper cases.

2. Place the butter, sugar and eggs in a bowl and then sift in the flour and baking powder. Finely grate the zest of the lemon into the bowl.

3. Beat together for about 2 minutes, preferably with an electric hand mixer, until pale and fluffy. Spoon into the paper cases and bake for 25 minutes for the larger cupcakes or 15 minutes for the fairy cakes until firm and golden. Cool on a wire rack.

4. To make the topping, cut the zest from the other lemon into thin strips and set aside.

5. Squeeze the juice from the lemon into a small saucepan. Add the sugar and heat gently until every grain of sugar has dissolved. Add the strips of zest and cool slightly. Spoon the syrup and lemon strips over the cupcakes while still warm. Leave to cool. Keep for up to 4 days in an airtight container.

HELPFUL HINT

As well as using lemon zest to add flavour to cakes, a concentrated lemon extract can be used. Extracts also come in a range of other fruit flavours and are usually sold in liquid form in small bottles.

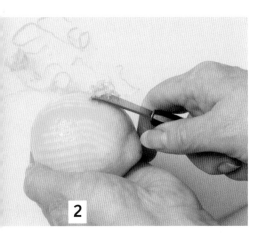

2

5

5

Mini Carrot Cupcakes

INGREDIENTS

Makes 22

175 g/6 oz self-raising
  wholemeal flour
1 tsp baking powder
½ tsp ground cinnamon
pinch salt
150 ml/¼ pint sunflower oil
150 g/5 oz soft light brown sugar
3 medium eggs, beaten
1 tsp vanilla extract
50 g/2 oz sultanas
225 g/8 oz carrots, peeled

To decorate:

1 orange
75 g/3 oz cream cheese
175 g/6 oz golden icing sugar

1 Preheat the oven to 180°C/350°F/Gas Mark 4. Lightly oil two 12-hole mini-muffin trays. Grate the carrots.

2 Sift the flour, baking powder, cinnamon and salt into a bowl, with any bran from the sieve.

3 Add the oil, sugar, eggs, vanilla extract, sultanas and grated carrots. Beat until smooth, then spoon into the muffin trays. Bake for about 20 minutes until risen and golden. Cool on a wire rack.

4 To decorate, peel thin strips of zest from the orange. Beat the cream cheese and icing sugar together with 2 tsp juice from the orange to make a spreading consistency. Swirl the icing over each cupcake and then top with shreds of orange zest. Keep for up to 3 days in an airtight container in a cool place.

HELPFUL HINT

A grater, for grating carrots, is a really good investment. It can also be used for grating citrus zests, chocolate and marzipan. Choose one with a fine and coarse side.

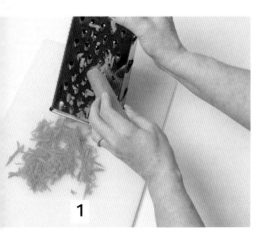

1

3

3

Chocolate & Cranberry Cupcakes

INGREDIENTS

Makes 12

125 g/4 oz soft margarine
125 g/4 oz golden caster sugar
2 medium eggs
175 g/6 oz self-raising flour
25 g/1 oz cocoa powder
1 tsp baking powder
2 tbsp milk
125 g/4 oz milk chocolate chips
50 g/2 oz dried cranberries

To decorate:

25 g/1 oz cocoa powder
40 g/1½ oz unsalted butter
125 g/4 oz golden icing sugar
25 g/1 oz dried cranberries

1 Preheat the oven to 180°C/350°F/Gas Mark 4. Line a muffin tray with 12 deep paper cases.

2 Place the margarine, sugar and eggs in a bowl, then sift in the flour, cocoa powder and baking powder.

3 Add the milk and beat until smooth, then fold in the chocolate chips and cranberries. Spoon into the paper cases and bake for 15–20 minutes until firm in the centre. Remove to a wire rack to cool.

4 To decorate the cupcakes, blend the cocoa powder with 1 tablespoon hot water until smooth. Cool for 5 minutes. Beat the butter and icing sugar together and then beat in the cocoa mixture.

5 Place in a piping bag with a plain nozzle and pipe swirls on top of each cupcake. Top with dried cranberries. Keep for 2–3 days in the refrigerator.

FOOD FACT

Dried cranberries are quite a lot cheaper than fresh ones, and they make a great store-cupboard ingredient, since they keep so well.

2

3

3

Sticky Toffee Cupcakes

INGREDIENTS

Makes 16–18

50 g/5 oz stoned dates
1 tsp bicarbonate of soda
250 ml/8 fl oz hot water
175 g/6 oz plain flour
1 tsp baking powder
50 g/2 oz butter or block
  margarine, diced
200 g/7 oz soft light brown sugar
1 large egg, beaten
½ tsp vanilla extract

For the icing:

25 g/1 oz unsalted butter
5 tbsp soft light brown sugar
4 tbsp double cream

1 Preheat the oven to 180°C/350°F/Gas Mark 4. Line one or two bun trays with 16–18 fairy-cake cases, depending on the depth of the tray holes. Chop the dates, then place in a bowl with the bicarbonate of soda and pour over the hot water. Stir, then set aside to cool.

2 Sift the flour and baking powder into a bowl and add the diced butter. Rub in between your fingertips until the mixture resembles fine crumbs. Stir in the sugar and mix well. Add the egg, vanilla extract and the date mixture. Beat with a wooden spoon until smooth.

3 Spoon into the cases and bake for about 25 minutes until well risen and firm to the touch in the centre. Leave to cool in the tins for 5 minutes, then turn out to cool on a wire rack.

4 To make the topping, place the butter, sugar and cream in a small pan over a low heat and stir until the sugar dissolves. Bring to the boil and boil for 1–2 minutes until the mixture thickens. Brush quickly over each fairy cake, as the mixture will set as it cools. Keep for up to 2 days in an airtight container.

FOOD FACT

Dried dates come in dried blocks, which need to be soaked in water before use, or semi-dried or soft and ready to eat. They are great for adding a sweet sticky consistency to all types of cake.

1

1

2

Almond & Cherry Cupcakes with Rosewater Icing

INGREDIENTS

Makes 12

50 g/2 oz glacé cherries, plus extra
   for decoration
125 g/4 oz self-raising flour, plus extra
   to dust
125 g/4 oz soft margarine
125 g/4 oz caster sugar
2 medium eggs
½ tsp almond extract

To decorate:

125 g/4 oz icing sugar
1 tsp lemon juice
pink food colouring
1 tbsp rosewater essence

1   Preheat the oven to 190°C/375°F/Gas Mark 5. Line a 12-hole bun tray with small paper cases. Wash the glacé cherries, then dry them thoroughly. Chop the cherries, then dust lightly in flour and set aside.

2   Sift the flour into a bowl, then add the margarine, sugar, eggs and extract. Beat until smooth for about 2 minutes, then fold in the chopped cherries.

3   Spoon into the paper cases. Bake for 15–20 minutes until golden and springy in the centre. Turn out to cool on a wire rack.

4   To decorate, mix the icing sugar with the lemon juice, rosewater essence and 2 tsp water to form a smooth glacé icing. Add a little pink food colouring and drizzle over the top of each cupcake. Place a halved cherry on top and leave to set for 30 minutes. Keep for 2–3 days in an airtight container.

TASTY TIP

Rosewater can be used for flavouring both cake mixtures and icing. It has a delicate, perfumed flavour and will give your cakes a fresh, fruity twist.

1

1

2

Shaggy Coconut Cupcakes

INGREDIENTS

Makes 12

¹/₂ tsp baking powder
200 g/7 oz self-raising flour
175 g/6 oz caster sugar
2 tbsp desiccated coconut
175 g/6 oz soft margarine
3 medium eggs, beaten
2 tbsp milk

To decorate:

1 batch buttercream
1 tbsp coconut liqueur (optional)
175 g/6 oz large shredded
   coconut strands

1 Preheat the oven to 180°C/350°F/Gas Mark 4. Line a 12-hole deep muffin tray with paper cases.

2 Sift the baking powder and flour into a large bowl. Add all the remaining ingredients and beat for about 2 minutes until smooth and creamy. Divide evenly between the paper cases.

3 Bake for 18–20 minutes until risen, golden and firm to the touch and a skewer inserted into the middle comes out clean. Leave in the muffin trays for 2 minutes, then turn out to cool on a wire rack.

4 To decorate the cupcakes, if you are using the coconut liqueur, beat this into the buttercream and then swirl over each cupcake. To decorate, press large strands of shredded coconut into the buttercream. Keep for up to 3 days in an airtight container in a cool place.

FOOD FACT

Coconut comes in many varieties. Powdery, sweet dessicated coconut comes as a fine powder that can be put into cake mixtures, while dried coconut slices make a really delicious cake topping.

Coffee & Walnut Fudge Cupcakes

INGREDIENTS

Makes 16–18

125 g/4 oz self-raising flour
125 g/4 oz butter, softened
125 g/ 4 oz golden caster sugar
2 medium eggs, beaten
1 tbsp golden syrup
50 g/2 oz walnuts, finely chopped

To decorate:
225 g/8 oz golden icing sugar
125 g/4 oz unsalted butter, softened
2 tsp coffee extract
16–18 small walnut pieces

1 Preheat the oven to 200°C/400°F/Gas Mark 6. Line two 12-hole bun trays with 16–18 small foil cases, depending on the depth of the tray holes.

2 Stir the flour into a bowl and add the butter, sugar, eggs and syrup. Beat for about 2 minutes, then fold in the walnuts.

3 Spoon the mixture into the paper cases and bake for about 12–14 minutes until well risen and springy in the centre. Remove to a wire rack to cool.

4 Make the frosting by sifting the icing sugar into a bowl. Add the butter, coffee extract and 1 tablespoon hot water. Beat until light and fluffy, then place in a piping bag fitted with a star nozzle. Pipe a swirl on each cupcake and top with a walnut piece. Keep for 3–4 days in an airtight container in a cool place.

FOOD FACT
Golden icing sugar is simply another name for unrefined icing sugar. Like unrefined sugar, it has a lovely rich colour and flavour.

1

2

4

Madeleine Cupcakes

INGREDIENTS

Makes 10–12

125 g/4 oz self-raising flour
125 g/4 oz butter, softened
125 g/4 oz golden caster sugar
2 medium eggs, beaten
1 tsp vanilla extract

To decorate:

4 tbsp seedless raspberry jam
65 g/2½ oz desiccated coconut
glacé cherries, halved

1 Preheat the oven to 180°C/350°F/Gas Mark 4. Line a 12-hole muffin tray with 10–12 paper cases, depending on the depth of the holes.

2 Sift the flour into a bowl and add the butter, sugar, eggs and extract. Beat for about 2 minutes until smooth, then spoon into the paper cases.

3 Bake in the centre of the oven for about 14–16 minutes until well risen and springy in the centre. Transfer to a wire rack to cool.

4 To decorate the cupcakes, warm the raspberry jam in a small pan or in the microwave oven in a heatproof dish on low for a few seconds. Brush the warmed jam over the top of each cupcake. Lightly coat the top of each cupcake with coconut, then finish with a halved cherry. Keep for up to 3 days in an airtight container.

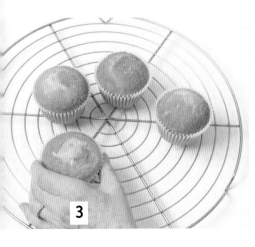

3

4

4

Lamington Cupcakes

INGREDIENTS

Makes 12

125 g/4 oz self-raising flour
125 g/4 oz butter, softened
125 g/4 oz golden caster sugar
2 medium eggs, beaten
1 tsp vanilla extract

To decorate:

350 g/12 oz caster sugar
1 tbsp cocoa powder
125 ml/4 fl oz water
65 g/2½ oz desiccated coconut
ready-made chocolate decorations

HELPFUL HINT

Ready-made cake decorations can be bought in supermarkets, or by mail order from specialist cake decorating companies, and are a quick and easy way to make your cakes look really special.

1 Preheat the oven to 180°C/350°F/Gas Mark 4. Line a 12-hole muffin tray with deep paper cases.

2 Sift the flour into a bowl and add the butter, sugar, eggs and vanilla extract. Beat for about 2 minutes until smooth, then spoon into the paper cases.

3 Bake in the centre of the oven for about 18 minutes until well risen and springy in the centre. Transfer to a wire rack to cool.

4 To make the icing, place the caster sugar, cocoa powder and water in a large heavy-based pan.

5 Heat over a low heat until every grain of sugar has dissolved. Bring to the boil and then simmer for about 6 minutes, without stirring, until thickened into syrup. Pour into a bowl and use the syrup while it is still hot, as it will set as it cools.

6 Place the coconut into a large bowl. Dip the top of each cupcake into the hot chocolate syrup to coat the top, then dip in coconut, decorate and place on a tray to dry. Keep for 2–3 days in an airtight container.

4

5

6

Mini Cupcakes

INGREDIENTS

Makes 24

100 g/3½ oz golden caster sugar
100 g/3½ oz butter, softened
finely grated zest of ½ lemon and
  1 tsp juice
2 medium eggs, beaten
100 g/3½ oz self-raising flour

To decorate:

50 g/2 oz unsalted butter, softened
1 tsp vanilla extract
125 g/4 oz icing sugar, sifted
1 tbsp milk
paste food colourings
sugar sprinkles

1 Preheat the oven to 190°C/375°F/Gas Mark 5. Line a 24-hole mini-muffin tray with mini paper muffin cases.

2 Put the sugar, butter and lemon zest in a large bowl and beat until light and fluffy. Beat in the eggs a little at a time, adding a teaspoon of flour with each addition. Fold in the rest of the flour and the lemon juice and mix until smooth.

3 Spoon into the mini muffin cases and bake for about 12 minutes until golden and risen. Transfer to a wire rack to cool.

4 To make the icing, beat the butter and vanilla extract together until light and fluffy, then gradually beat in the icing sugar and milk until a soft, easy-to-spread consistency has formed. Colour the icing in batches with paste food colourings, then spread over the cold cupcakes with a flat-bladed knife. Decorate with sugar sprinkles. Keep in an airtight container for up to 2 days.

TASTY TIP

Making cupcakes in different colours is great fun! A good idea is to theme the colours for different celebrations. Red, white and green, for example, at Christmas, or the colours of your national flag during the World Cup.

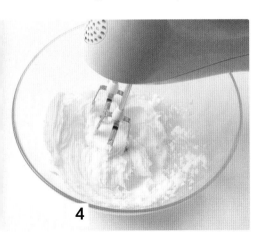

4

4

4

Raspberry Butterfly Cupcakes

INGREDIENTS

Makes 12–14

125 g/4 oz caster sugar
125 g/4 oz soft tub margarine
2 medium eggs
125 g/4 oz self-raising flour
½ tsp baking powder
½ tsp vanilla extract

To decorate:

4 tbsp seedless raspberry jam
12–14 fresh raspberries
icing sugar, to dust

1 Preheat the oven to 190°C/375°F/Gas Mark 5. Line one or two bun trays with 12–14 paper cases, depending on the depth of the holes.

2 Place all the cupcake ingredients in a large bowl and beat with an electric mixer for about 2 minutes until smooth. Fill the paper cases halfway up with the mixture.

3 Bake for about 15 minutes until firm, risen and golden. Remove to a wire rack to cool.

4 When cold, cut a small circle out of the top of each cupcake and then cut the circle in half to form wings.

5 Fill each cupcake with a teaspoon of raspberry jam. Replace the wings at an angle and top each with a fresh raspberry. Dust lightly with icing sugar and serve immediately.

HELPFUL HINT

Many cupcakes will form a small peak while baking and this is an ideal shape for coating with buttercream or icing. Some cupcakes, though, require a flat top to decorate – use a sharp knife to trim the top so it is flat.

3

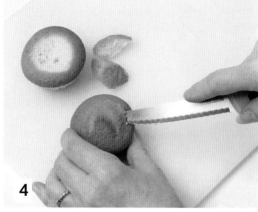

4

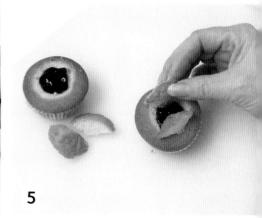

5

Strawberry Swirl Cupcakes

INGREDIENTS

Makes 12

125 g/4 oz caster sugar
125 g/4 oz soft tub margarine
2 medium eggs
125 g/4 oz self-raising flour
½ tsp baking powder
2 tbsp sieved strawberry jam

To decorate:

50 g/2 oz unsalted butter, softened
300 g/11 oz icing sugar, sifted
125 g/4 oz full-fat cream cheese
1 tbsp sieved strawberry jam
pink food colouring

1 Preheat the oven to 190°C/375°F/Gas Mark 5. Line a muffin tray with 12 deep paper cases.

2 Place all the cupcake ingredients except the jam in a large bowl and beat with an electric mixer for about 2 minutes until smooth. Fill the paper cases halfway up with the mixture.

3 Add ½ teaspoon jam to each case and swirl it into the mixture. Bake for about 15 minutes until firm, risen and golden. Remove to a wire rack to cool.

4 To prepare the frosting, beat the butter until soft, then gradually add the icing sugar until the mixture is light. Add the cream cheese and whisk until light and fluffy.

5 Divide the mixture in half and beat the strawberry jam and pink food colouring into one half. Fit a piping bag with a wide star nozzle and spoon strawberry cream on one side of the bag and the plain cream on the other. Pipe swirls on top of the cupcakes. Keep for up to 3 days in an airtight container in a cool place.

FOOD FACT

You can buy food colourings in the form of a liquid, paste, gel, powder or dust. A huge range of colours is available.

4

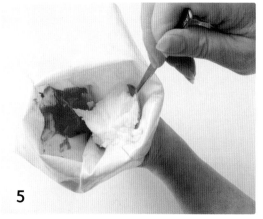

5

5

Double Cherry Cupcakes

INGREDIENTS

Makes 12 large cupcakes or 18 fairy cakes

50 g/2 oz glacé cherries
125 g/4 oz self-raising flour
25 g/1 oz dried morello cherries
125 g/4 oz soft margarine
125 g/4 oz caster sugar
2 medium eggs
$\frac{1}{2}$ tsp almond extract

To decorate:

125 g/4 oz fondant icing sugar
pale pink liquid food colouring
40 g/1$\frac{1}{2}$ oz glacé cherries

FOOD FACT

Glacé cherries are usually sold thinly coated in syrup. They keep well in their tubs, stored in a cool place. You should always wash the syrup off the cherries before you use them.

1 Preheat the oven to 190°C/375°F/Gas Mark 5. Line a 12-hole muffin tray with deep paper cases, or two trays with 18 fairy-cake cases. Wash the cherries, dry on absorbent kitchen paper and chop.

2 Dust the chopped glacé cherries lightly in a tablespoon of the flour, then mix with the morello cherries and set aside. Sift the rest of the flour into a bowl, then add the margarine, sugar, eggs and almond extract. Beat for about 2 minutes until smooth, then fold in the cherries.

3 Spoon the batter into the paper cases and bake for 15–20 minutes until well risen and springy in the centre. Turn out to cool on a wire rack.

4 To decorate the cupcakes, trim the tops level. Mix the icing sugar with 2–3 teaspoons warm water and a few drops pink food colouring to make a thick consistency. Spoon the icing over each cupcake, filling right up to the edge.

5 Chop the cherries finely and sprinkle over the icing. Leave to set for 30 minutes. Keep for up to 3 days in an airtight container.

1

2

2

Lemon & Ginger Cupcakes

INGREDIENTS

Makes 18

8 tbsp golden syrup
125 g/4 oz block margarine
225 g/8 oz plain flour
2 tsp ground ginger
75 g/3 oz sultanas
50 g/2 oz soft dark brown sugar
200 ml/7 fl oz milk
1 tsp bicarbonate of soda
1 medium egg, beaten

To decorate:

125 g/4 oz golden icing sugar
1 tsp lemon juice
glacé ginger pieces

1 Preheat the oven to 180°C/350°F/Gas Mark 4. Line two shallow muffin trays with 18 paper cases.

2 Place the syrup and margarine in a heavy-based pan and melt together gently.

3 Sift the flour and ginger into a bowl, then stir in the sultanas and sugar. Warm the milk and stir in the bicarbonate of soda.

4 Pour the syrup mixture, milk and beaten egg into the dry ingredients and beat until smooth. Pour the mixture into a jug.

5 Carefully spoon 2 tbsp of the mixture into each case (the mixture will be wet). Bake for about 30 minutes. Cool in the tins for 10 minutes, then turn out to cool on a wire rack.

6 To decorate, blend the icing sugar with the lemon juice and 1 tbsp warm water to make a thin glacé icing. Drizzle over the top of each cupcake, then top with glacé ginger pieces. Leave to set for 30 minutes. Keep in an airtight container for up to 5 days.

FOOD FACT

Ginger comes in a sticky glacé variety or in a dried crystallised form, coated in sugar crystals. Both types can be used mixed into a cake mixture or as decoration.

2

3

3

Crystallised Violet Cupcakes

INGREDIENTS

Makes 12

150 g/5 oz butter, softened
150 g/5 oz caster sugar
3 medium eggs, beaten
150 g/5 oz self-raising flour
½ tsp baking powder
1 lemon

To decorate:

12 fresh violets
1 egg white
caster sugar, for dusting
125 g/4 oz fondant icing sugar
pale violet food colouring

1 Preheat the oven to 180°C/350°F/Gas Mark 4 and line a 12-hole muffin tray with deep paper cases.

2 Place the butter, sugar and eggs in a bowl. Sift in the flour and baking powder. Finely grate in the zest from the lemon.

3 Beat together for about 2 minutes with an electric hand mixer until pale and fluffy. Spoon into the paper cases and bake for 20–25 minutes until firm and golden. Cool on a wire rack.

4 To decorate the cupcakes, spread the violets on some nonstick baking parchment. Beat the egg white until frothy, then brush thinly over the violets. Dust with caster sugar and leave to dry out for 2 hours.

5 Beat the icing sugar with the colouring and enough water to give a thin coating consistency. Drizzle over the top of each cupcake quickly and top with a violet. Leave to set for 30 minutes. Store in an airtight container in a cool place. Keep for up to 2 days.

FOOD FACT

Caster sugar, fine granulated sugar, is a key ingredient for cake making. It is useful for dusting cakes, as a way to finish them, and also mixes well with butter and margarine when making cake mixtures.

4

4

5

Cream Cheese Pastel Swirls

INGREDIENTS

Makes 12

150 g/5 oz butter, softened
150 g/5 oz caster sugar
3 medium eggs
1 tsp vanilla extract
175 g/6 oz self-raising flour

To decorate:

1 batch cream cheese frosting
Paste food colourings

1. Preheat the oven to 180°C/350°F/Gas Mark 4. Line a 12-hole muffin tray with deep paper cases.

2. Place the butter and sugar in a bowl and cream together. In another bowl, beat the eggs with the vanilla extract.

3. Sift the flour into the creamed mixture, then beat in the eggs until smooth. Spoon into the cases, filling them three-quarters full.

4. Bake for about 18 minutes until firm to the touch in the centre. Turn out to cool on a wire rack.

5. Divide the frosting into three batches. Colour one green and one pink with dots of food colouring and leave one batch plain. Place each batch in a piping bag fitted with a star nozzle and pipe large swirls on top of each cupcake. Keep for up to 3 days in an airtight container in a cool place.

HELPFUL HINT

If you are going to make lots of cupcakes, it might be worth investing in an electric mixer. It will make really short work of whisking butter and sugar, key ingredients for cupcakes.

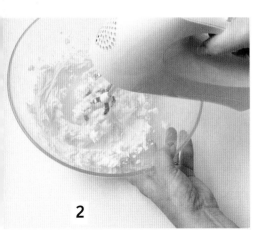

2

3

5

Daisy Chain Lemon Cupcakes

INGREDIENTS

Makes 12

125 g/4 oz caster sugar
125 g/4 oz soft tub margarine
2 medium eggs
125 g/4 oz self-raising flour
½ tsp baking powder
1 tsp lemon juice

To decorate:

50 g/2 oz ready-to-roll sugarpaste
yellow piping icing tube
225 g/8 oz fondant icing sugar
lemon yellow food colouring

1 Preheat the oven to 190°C/375°F/Gas Mark 5. Line a bun tray with 12 paper cases.

2 Place all the cupcake ingredients in a large bowl and beat with an electric mixer for about 2 minutes until smooth. Fill the paper cases halfway up with the mixture.

3 Bake for about 15 minutes until firm, risen and golden. Remove to a wire rack to cool.

4 Roll out the icing thinly and stamp out small daisies with a fluted daisy cutter. Pipe a small yellow dot of icing into the centre of each and leave to dry out for 1 hour.

5 Blend the fondant icing sugar with a little water and a few dots of yellow colouring to make a thick, easy-to-spread icing, then smooth over the top of each cupcake. Decorate with the cut-out daisies immediately and leave to set for 1 hour. Keep for up to 3 days in an airtight container.

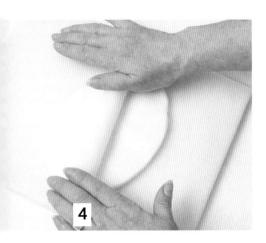

4

4

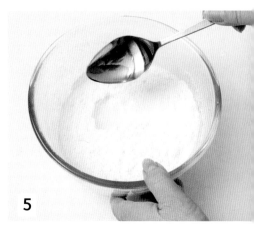

5

Florentine-topped Cupcakes

INGREDIENTS

Makes 18

150 g/5 oz butter, softened
150 g/5 oz caster sugar
175 g/6 oz self-raising flour
3 medium eggs
1 tsp vanilla extract
75 g/3 oz glacé cherries, chopped
50 g/2 oz angelica, chopped
50 g/2 oz candied peel, chopped
50 g/2 oz dried cranberries

To decorate:

75 g/3 oz plain or milk
  chocolate, melted
50 g/2 oz flaked almonds

FOOD FACT

Almonds can be bought in whole, flaked, chopped and ground varieties. Shelled almonds come with the skins on. The skins can be removed by immersing the nuts in boiling water for a couple of minutes, then plunging them into cold water. The skins should then slip off easily.

1 Preheat the oven to 180°C/350°F/Gas Mark 4. Line two 12-hole muffin trays with 18 paper cases.

2 Place the butter and sugar in a bowl, then sift in the flour. In another bowl, beat the eggs with the vanilla extract, then add to the first mixture and beat until smooth.

3 Fold in half the cherries, angelica, peel and cranberries. Spoon into the cases, filling them three-quarters full.

4 Bake for about 18 minutes until firm to the touch in the centre. Turn out to cool on a wire rack.

5 Spoon a little melted chocolate on top of each cupcake, then scatter the remaining cherries, angelica, peel and cranberries and the almonds into the wet chocolate. Drizzle the remaining chocolate over the fruit topping with a teaspoon and leave to set for 30 minutes. Keep for up to 2 days in an airtight container.

2

3

3

Fondant Fancies

INGREDIENTS

Makes 16–18

150 g/5 oz self-raising flour
150 g/5 oz caster sugar
50 g/2 oz ground almonds
150 g/5 oz butter, softened
3 medium eggs, beaten
4 tbsp milk

To decorate:

450 g/1 lb fondant icing sugar
paste food colourings
selection fancy cake decorations

1 Preheat the oven to 180°C/350°F/Gas Mark 4. Line two 12-hole bun trays with 16–18 paper cases, depending on the depth of the tray holes.

2 Sift the flour into a bowl and stir in the caster sugar and almonds. Add the butter, eggs and milk and beat until smooth.

3 Spoon into the paper cases and bake for 15–20 minutes until golden and firm to the touch. Turn out to cool on a wire rack. When cool, trim the tops flat if they have peaked slightly.

4 To decorate the cupcakes, make the fondant icing to a thick coating consistency, following the packet instructions. Divide into batches and colour each separately with a little paste food colouring. Keep each bowl covered with a damp cloth until needed. Spoon some icing over each cupcake, being sure to flood it right to the edge. Top each with a fancy decoration and leave to set for 30 minutes. Keep for up to 2 days in a cool place.

2

4

4

Lemon & Cardamom Cupcakes with Mascarpone Topping

INGREDIENTS

Makes 12

1 tsp cardamom seeds
200 g/7 oz butter
50 g/2 oz plain flour
200 g/7 oz self-raising flour
1 tsp baking powder
200 g/7 oz caster sugar
zest of 1 lemon, finely grated
3 medium eggs
100 ml/3½ fl oz natural yogurt
4 tbsp lemon curd

To decorate:

250 g/9 oz tub mascarpone
6 tbsp icing sugar
1 tsp lemon juice
lemon zest strips

TASTY TIP

Spices, such as cardamom, can bring a whole new world of flavour to cupcakes. They can be bought cheaply from ethnic food shops. To keep their flavour, you should store in glass jars, out of the light.

1 Preheat the oven to 180°C/350°F/Gas Mark 4. Line a 12-hole muffin tray with deep paper cases. Crush the cardamom seeds and remove the outer cases. Melt the butter and leave aside to cool.

2 Sift the flours and baking powder into a bowl and stir in the crushed seeds, sugar and lemon zest.

3 In another bowl, whisk together the eggs and yogurt. Pour into the dry ingredients with the cooled melted butter and beat until combined.

4 Divide half the mixture between the paper cases, put a teaspoon of lemon curd into each, then top with the remaining mixture. Bake for about 25 minutes until golden.

5 To make the topping, beat the mascarpone with the icing sugar and lemon juice. Swirl onto each cupcake and top with lemon strips. Eat fresh on day of baking once decorated or store, undecorated, in an airtight container for up to 2 days and add the topping just before serving.

1

1

4

Pink Butterfly Cupcakes

INGREDIENTS

Makes 12

150 g/5 oz butter, softened
150 g/5 oz caster sugar
3 medium eggs, beaten
1 tsp vanilla extract
150 g/5 oz self-raising flour
½ tsp baking powder

To decorate:

pink and brown paste food colouring
225 g/8 oz ready-to-roll sugarpaste
1 batch cream cheese frosting
Tubes of gel writing icing

HELPFUL HINT

Pastry cutters come in all shapes and sizes, so the only limit to how you design your cupcakes is your imagination. For example, use a star-shaped cutter and orange and black colouring to make cupcakes with an outer space design! Kids, especially, love designing cupcakes so get them involved too.

1 Preheat the oven to 180°C/350°F/Gas Mark 4 and line a 12-hole muffin tray with deep paper cases.

2 Place the butter, sugar, eggs and vanilla extract in a bowl and then sift in the flour and baking powder. Beat together for about 2 minutes with an electric hand mixer until pale and fluffy. Spoon into the paper cases and bake for 20–25 minutes until firm and golden. Cool on a wire rack.

3 To decorate the cupcakes, colour 200 g/7 oz of the sugarpaste pale pink and colour the remainder brown. Roll out the sugarpaste thinly and, using a cutter, template or freehand, cut out four petal shapes for the wings for each cupcake and set them on nonstick baking parchment or clingfilm. Cut out 48 shapes altogether and leave to dry flat until firm (about 2 hours). Colour the cream cheese frosting bright pink and place in a piping bag fitted with a star nozzle.

4 Pipe a swirl of pink icing to cover the top of each cupcake and then press four wings on top of each. Mould the brown icing into a thin body shape and place on each cupcake. Pipe dots on the wings with tubes of gel writing icing. Keep for up to 2 days in an airtight container in a cool place.

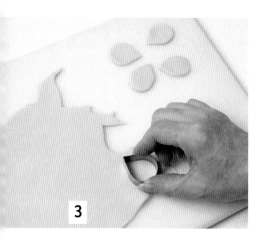

3

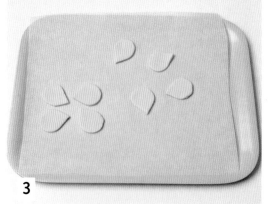

3

4

Rocky Road Cupcakes

INGREDIENTS

Makes 14–18

125 g/4 oz self-raising flour
25 g/1 oz cocoa powder
125 g/4 oz soft dark brown sugar
125 g/4 oz soft margarine
2 medium eggs, beaten
2 tbsp milk

To decorate:

75 g/3 oz dark chocolate, broken into
   squares
40 g/1½ oz butter
75 g/3 oz mini marshmallows
40 g/1½ oz chopped mixed nuts

1 Preheat the oven to 180°C/350°F/Gas Mark 4. Line two bun trays with 14–18 paper cases or silicone cupcake moulds, depending on the depth of the holes.

2 Sift the flour and cocoa powder into a large bowl. Add the sugar, margarine, eggs and milk and whisk with an electric beater for about 2 minutes until smooth.

3 Divide the mixture evenly between the paper cases and bake for about 20 minutes until a skewer inserted into the middle comes out clean. Remove the tray from the oven, but leave the oven on.

4 To make the topping, gently melt the chocolate and butter together in a small pan over a low heat. Place the melted chocolate mixture in an icing bag made of greaseproof paper and snip away the end. Pipe a little of the mixture on top of each cupcake, then scatter the marshmallows and nuts over each one and return to the oven. Bake for 2–3 minutes to soften the marshmallows. Remove from the oven and pipe the remaining chocolate over the marshmallows. Leave to cool in the trays for 5 minutes, then remove to cool on a wire rack. Serve warm or cold. Keep for up to 2 days in an airtight container.

TASTY TIP

Anything with marshmallows will be a hit with your kids. If they have a sleepover with their friends, instead of serving marshmallows by themselves, why not bake these delicious cupcakes for them.

2

3

4

Cappuccino Cupcakes

INGREDIENTS

Makes 12–14

125 g/4 oz soft margarine
125 g/4 oz golden caster sugar
150 g/5 oz self-raising flour
2 tbsp cocoa powder
2 medium eggs
1 tbsp golden syrup
50 g/2 oz finely grated chocolate

To decorate:

150 ml/¼ pint double cream
½ tsp coffee extract
chocolate sprinkles

1   Preheat the oven to 180°C/350°F/Gas Mark 4. Line one or two bun trays with 12–14 paper cases or silicone moulds, depending on the depth of the holes.

2   Place the margarine and the sugar in a large bowl, then sift in the flour and cocoa powder.

3   In another bowl, beat the eggs with the syrup, then add to the flour mixture. Whisk together with an electric beater for 2 minutes, or by hand with a wooden spoon, until smooth and then fold in the grated chocolate.

4   Divide the mixture between the cases, filling them three-quarters full. Bake for about 20 minutes until springy to the touch in the centre. Turn out to cool on a wire rack.

5   To decorate, whisk the cream until it forms soft peaks, then whisk in the coffee extract. Swirl over the tops of the muffins with a small palette knife. Scatter the tops with chocolate sprinkles to serve. Eat on the day of decorating or keep for 1 day in a sealed container in the refrigerator.

TASTY TIP

Whether you buy ready-made chocolate sprinkles or make them yourself, you should buy the best-quality chocolate you can afford. Even cheaper supermarkets stock high-quality bars these days. You can make your own sprinkles by simply grating your chocolate along the coarse side of a grater.

3

5

5

Step-by-Step, Practical Recipes Cupcakes: Tips & Hints

Helpful Hint

Not only is baking cupcakes great fun, but it is a really great way to save some money – good quality, shop-bought cupcakes are quite expensive, so you will really see the difference in price if you bake them at home. On top of this, home-made cakes tend to be tastier and you can also decorate them according to your own style and taste.

Tasty Tip

To make sure your cupcakes are lovely and moist, and not too dry, make sure they are not baked too slowly, and that the mixture is not too dry – this happens if the cake mixture has not been rubbed in or beaten sufficiently. Cupcakes that are too dry tend to be crumbly when cut and go stale quite quickly.

Food Fact

The first mention of a cake that could be cooked in a cup can be traced as far back as 1796, though cupcakes' popularity took off in the early 1800s. Early 21st-century nostalgia has seen old-fashioned things becoming popular again – clothes, home furnishings and even cakes!

Helpful Hint

Paper cupcake cases come in many varieties, colours and shapes. It is best to buy the more expensive ones, which are thicker and give a good shape to the cake as it rises. Oil and moisture is less likely to penetrate through the thicker cases, whereas it may show through the cheaper ones. Metallic gold, silver and coloured cupcake cases give good results and create a stunning effect for a special occasion. Mini cupcake cases can also be found, though you will perhaps have to look online for these.

Helpful Hint

A nylon piping bag and a set of nozzles is a vital piece of equipment for lots of types of baking, but particularly so for cupcakes. Look for a set with a plain nozzle and various star nozzles for piping swirls around the cupcakes. The larger the star nozzle, the larger the swirls around the cupcake. Disposable paper or clear plastic icing bags are available, but nylon piping bags can be washed out in warm soapy water and dried out, ready to use again.

Helpful Hint

When storing cupcakes, make sure the cakes are completely cold, otherwise condensation can form in the container, causing the cakes to go mouldy. Large plastic food containers are ideal, as the cakes can be kept flat in one layer and will also stay moist.

Tasty Tip

Get your kids involved with baking cupcakes. They are a great place to start with baking, since children love how colourful they look and that they come in loads of different styles. Children also sometimes turn out some surprisingly delicious results, which is surely an incentive to get them baking! Teaching them to bake will also get them started with learning how to cook in general.

Tasty Tip

If your cupcakes have gone wrong, there are a number of ways to patch them up. If the cakes have burnt on the outside, then simply scrape away with a serrated knife and cover the surface with buttercream. If the cakes are a little dry, sweeten them up with a few drops of sweet sherry or orange juice!

Helpful Hint

Muffins trays, for cooking cupcakes, come in a variety of styles. Metal trays generally come with six or 12 deep-set holes. When you buy one of these you should buy the heaviest type you can – although they are expensive they will produce the best results as they distribute the heat more evenly. You should grease these trays with a little butter before use. Silicone trays also produce really good results. They are usually advertised as being nonstick, but it is still adviseable to grease them before cooking.

Food Fact

In the early 19th century, before muffin tins were available, cupcakes were made in individual pottery cups, ramekins or moulds – they took their name from the cups they were baked in. This name has endured and is now given to any small cake that is about the size of a teacup.

First published in 2012 by
FLAME TREE PUBLISHING LTD
Crabtree Hall, Crabtree Lane, Fulham,
London, SW6 6TY, United Kingdom
www.flametreepublishing.com

The CIP record for this book is available from the British Library • Printed in China

NOTE: Recipes using uncooked eggs should be avoided by infants, the elderly, pregnant women and anyone suffering from an illness.

18 17 16 15 14 13 12   10 9 8 7 6 5 4 3 2 1

ISBN: 978-0-85775-606-0

ACKNOWLEDGEMENTS: Authors: Catherine Atkinson, Juliet Barker, Gina Steer, Vicki Smallwood, Carol Tennant, Mari Mererid Williams, Elizabeth Wolf-Cohen and Simone Wright. Photography: Colin Bowling, Paul Forrester and Stephen Brayne. Home Economists and Stylists: Jacqueline Bellefontaine, Mandy Phipps, Vicki Smallwood and Penny Stephens. All props supplied by Barbara Stewart at Surfaces. Publisher and Creative Director: Nick Wells. Editorial: Catherine Taylor, Sarah Goulding, Marcus Hardie, Gina Steer and Karen Fitzpatrick. Design and Production: Chris Herbert, Mike Spender, Colin Rudderham and Helen Wall.